A Game of Skittles

Ramin and Emma were going
to have a game of skittles.

"Ramin, roll the ball at the skittles,"
said Emma.
"Then we will count
the number of skittles
that fall down."

"Let's have three games," said Ramin.

Ramin rolled the ball at the skittles.

The ball hit one

of the yellow skittles.

Crash!

It fell over.

And then two blue skittles

went down.

"I made three skittles fall over,"

said Ramin.

Ramin	Emma
3	

He put the number 3 on his card.

Ramin set up the skittles again.

"Now it's my turn," said Emma.

Emma rolled the ball at the skittles.
Five skittles went down.
Crash!

Emma shouted,
"I made five skittles fall down."

Ramin
3

Emma
5

She put the number 5 on her card.

Then Ramin rolled the ball
at the skittles.
The ball hit the red skittle.
It fell over.
And then four more skittles fell over.

He put the number 5 on his card.

Ramin

3 + 5

Emma

5

It was Emma's turn again.

Over went six skittles.

Crash!

She put the number 6 on her card.

Ramin

3 + 5

Emma

5 + 6

"This is my last turn," said Ramin.

The ball went very fast!
It hit the red skittle. **Crash!**
All the skittles fell down.

"I did it! I did it!" shouted Ramin.
"I got ten skittles."

Ramin	Emma
3 + 5 + 10	5 + 6

He put the number 10 on his card.

"Now it is **my** last turn," said Emma.

She made the ball go very fast, too. Over went nine skittles. **Crash!**

Emma put the number **9** on her card.

Ramin
3 + 5 + 10

Emma
5 + 6 + 9

Ramin and Emma added up their numbers.

Emma was the winner.

She had 20.

Ramin had 18.

20 is two more than 18.

Ramin ⑱
3 + 5 + 10

| 3 and 5 make 8 | $3 + 5 = 8$ |

8 and 10 more make 18 $8 + 10 = 18$

Emma ⑳
5 + 6 + 9

| 5 and 6 make 11 | $5 + 6 = 11$ |

11 and 9 more make 20 $11 + 9 = 20$